SIENESE
QUATTROCENTO
PAINTING

PHAIDON
PRESS

GIOVANNI DI PAOLO: ST. NICHOLAS OF TOLENTINO SAVING A SHIP AT SEA

JOHN G. JOHNSON ART COLLECTION, PHILADELPHIA

SIENESE
QUATTROCENTO
PAINTING

BY

JOHN POPE-HENNESSY

MCMXLVII
OXFORD & LONDON
PHAIDON PRESS LTD

MADE IN GREAT BRITAIN

1947

PRINTED IN GREAT BRITAIN BY ROBERT MACLEHOSE AND CO. LTD.

THE UNIVERSITY PRESS, GLASGOW

PREFACE

THIS book is an anthology of Sienese quattrocento paintings and not a history of quattrocento painting. In the belief that what is termed artistic personality is better represented by a small number of pictures reproduced in detail than by a large quantity of general photographs, many important works have been omitted in order that the photographs included in the book should communicate more fully a sense of contact with originals.

In war conditions the preparation of such a book would have been impossible without the assistance of museum authorities in Great Britain and the U.S.A. In this connection I am specially indebted to Sir Kenneth Clark, of the National Gallery, London, and to Mr. John Walker, of the National Gallery of Art, Washington, as well as to Professor T. S. Bodkin, of the Barber Institute at Birmingham; Mr. W. G. Constable, of the Boston Museum of Fine Arts; Mr. Horace Jayne, of the Metropolitan Museum, New York; Mr. S. C. Kaines-Smith, of the Cook Collection; Mr. Frank Lambert, of the Walker Art Gallery, Liverpool; and Mr. Daniel Catton Rich, of the Art Institute of Chicago: all of whom have responded to requests for detail photographs of paintings in their galleries. I am also indebted to Mr. Ludwig Goldscheider, Mr. Christopher Norris and Mr. Edward Hutton for the loan of photographs; to Conte Alessandro Contini-Bonacossi and Miss Helen C. Frick for permission to reproduce the photographs on Plates I-V and XX; to Mr. Edward Fowles for the photographs on Plate LXXIX and Fig. 20; to Mr. Germain Seligmann for the photographs on Plates LXXXIX-XCII; to Mr. Otto Fein, of the Warburg Institute, for the excellent photographs on Plates XLV-VII; and to that invaluable institution, the Frick Art Reference Library, for the photographs on Plates XL-III, LIV, LXI-V.

In the interests of readability I have omitted all references from the text and notes, and I feel bound to add, for the information of those who wish to pursue the study of the quattrocento in Siena, a brief note on the literature of Sienese painting. Among the general introductions to Italian painting which contain chapters on the Sienese achievement pride of place is taken by Berenson's unrivalled Italian Painters of the Renaissance (London, 1932). Also noteworthy is the admirable introduction with which Langton Douglas prefaced the catalogue of the exhibition of Sienese art held at the Burlington Fine Arts Club in 1904. Van Marle's account of the activity of specific artists (The Development of the Italian Schools of Painting, The Hague, vols. ix and xvi), though valuable for its wealth of illustrations, is less systematic than that of Edgell (A History of Sienese Painting, New York, 1932).

Monographs have been devoted to most of the artists represented in this book. The best short account of Sassetta remains Berenson's A Sienese Painter of the Franciscan Legend (London, 1909). This may be supplemented with my own monograph on the artist (Sassetta, London, 1939). On Giovanni di Paolo the only available volume is my own (Giovanni di Paolo, London, 1937). The work of Sano di Pietro has been covered by Truebner (Die stilistische Entwicklung der Tafelbilder des Sano di Pietro, Strasbourg, 1925) in a short and able, though rather academic, book. A volume on Domenico di Bartolo by Wagner (Domenico di Bartolo Ghezzi, Göttingen, 1897-8) has been overtaken by recent research, and the most readily accessible account of Domenico's style is contained in two articles of my own in The Burlington Magazine for May and June, 1944. On Vecchietta the best monograph is that by Vigni (Lorenzo di Pietro detto il Vecchietta, Florence, 1937), while on Matteo di Giovanni there is a painstaking volume by Hartlaub (Matteo da Siena und seine Zeit, Strassburg, 1910). Selwyn Brinton's Francesco di Giorgio Martini of Siena (London, 1934) has been superseded by a comprehensive volume by Allen Weller (Francesco di Giorgio, Chicago, 1943). Cozzarelli is the subject of an interesting essay by Berenson (Essays in the Study of Sienese Painting, New York, 1918), and Neroccio of two articles by Dami (Rassegna d'Arte, 1918). The work of Benvenuto di Giovanni has not been seriously analysed.

J. P.-H.

SIENESE PAINTING IN THE FIFTEENTH CENTURY

The paintings illustrated in this book were executed in a single century in one and the same town in Italy. But the artists who painted them have more in common than the place or period in which they worked, for Sienese painting in the fifteenth century is marked by a general uniformity of manner, and by aesthetic and literary aspirations distinct from those of other schools. With few exceptions Sienese quattrocento paintings are decorative and two-dimensional. Sassetta's *Scenes from the Life of St. Anthony the Abbot* (Plates VI-VIII), completed in the first half of the century, and Neroccio's altarpiece (Plates XC-XCIII), painted towards its close, are reduced to a flat, linear pattern, which has no reference to physical reality; and where, in the *Assumption* of Matteo di Giovanni (Plates LVI-LX), a third dimension obtrudes itself, we are confronted not with solid forms, but with a system of modelling in relief, which recalls the effect of a wax portrait fixed to a flat ground. Sienese quattrocento painting makes no endeavour to instil in the spectator a sense of the material existence of the scenes it represents or to create an image which will survive scrutiny by prosaic eyes. Indeed the place of the Sienese achievement within the complex of Italian quattrocento painting may be compared to that of symbolist poetry in the twentieth century, in that its constituents are not unskilled or unsuccessful efforts to represent reality, but symbols of a supernatural world.

The outward appearance of Siena has changed little since the time at which these paintings were produced. Driving along the road from Florence, lit by the fireflies which Ruskin, as he approached the city, observed 'moving like fine broken starlight through the purple leaves', we see Siena, with its pink walls, its russet coloured towers, its white Cathedral, rise before us much as it must have risen before travellers in the quattrocento (Fig. 1). From the Cathedral the houses still, as in the days of Montaigne, decline to

FIG. 1. *Francesco di Giorgio: The City of Siena (Archivio di Stato, Siena)*

(7)

the curved Campo, 'a fine expanse, which slopes from all sides towards the palace, which in itself forms one of the segments of the circle somewhat less curved than the rest'. Its great conventual churches, its gateways, its public buildings remain intact, and the Siena of today is the same indolent, gay city, which Taine could describe as the Pompeii of the Middle Ages, and where Peter Beckford could note in his journal, 'Love, which is said to be the amusement of men and the business of women, is here, I think, the business of both'.

More, possibly, than that of any other school, Sienese quattrocento painting has its roots in the preceding century. In Florence the painting of the middle of the fifteenth century was regarded as superior to, and indeed as superseding, that of the painters of the earlier trecento. In Siena, on the other hand, the quattrocento was distinguished by an almost superstitious reverence for the painting of the fourteenth century. Some indication of the essential difference between the outlook of the Florentine artist, with his deep seated belief in artistic evolution, and of the Sienese, for whom the past formed a challenge rather than a heritage, may be found in the *Commentarii* of Ghiberti, who records in a tone midway between disapproval and surprise the conviction of his Sienese contemporaries that Simone Martini remained to their own day the supreme master of the school. In these circumstances it is not surprising that about 1450 Simone Martini's *Annunciation* of 1333 should have been adapted in the form of a free copy by an unknown artist for the chapel of the Compagnia della Morte, and that at least one small *Madonna of Humility* produced in the orbit of Simone Martini in the first half of the fourteenth century should have been reproduced again during the first half of the quattrocento.

Still more significant than this use of trecento motifs is the fact that fifteenth-century Sienese artists persistently adhered to the technical procedure of the painters of the fourteenth century. The use throughout the fifteenth century of the gold ground peculiar to trecento altarpieces is the most signal instance of this archaising tendency, and it was this rather than any other feature of Sienese quattrocento style that impeded the adoption by Sienese studios of the quasi-scientific representation of space, which became the rule in Florence relatively early in the century. Thus in Francesco di Giorgio's *Annunciation* (Plate LXXV), painted about 1470, we find perspective treated in a spirit of irrational fantasy, and in Matteo di Giovanni's *Madonna and Child with SS. John Baptist and Michael* of about 1490 in the Barber Institute at Birmingham (Plate LV) we have a composition in which three heads are shown on a gold ground with no explicit indication of the spatial relationship between them.

Moreover, the conditions under which painters in Siena worked were conducive to a less progressive and more sophisticated type of painting than that evolved in Florence. Throughout the fifteenth century it is the fresco that forms the unit of Florentine art. Between Masaccio's work in the Brancacci Chapel early in the quattrocento and Ghirlandaio's frescoes in S. Maria Novella towards its close, the century is punctuated by fresco cycles, whose naturalistic treatment was transmitted to work in smaller forms. If we search in Siena for an equivalent to the Cappella Bocchineri at Prato, to the choir of S. Egidio, or to the Villa Legnaia, we shall seek in vain, and it is by no means a coincidence that the only Sienese fresco cycle in the entire fifteenth century which is comparable to the naturalistic frescoes of Florentine artists, Domenico di Bartolo's scenes in the Pellegrinaio (Figs. 15 and 16), was commissioned by a rector with Florentine connections as propaganda for the hospital which he controlled. Instead in Siena the emphasis was on small, highly wrought and richly decorated panels, the affinities of which lie less with Florence than with the court art of North Italy.

The political history of Siena during the quattrocento does something to explain this fact. When the century opens, we find Siena under the suzerainty of the Duke of Milan, who 'regarded the Sienese more in the light of comrades and friends than of subjects or vassals', and when it closes, the city is in the grasp of the tyrant Pandolfo Petrucci. A Ghibelline state, Siena, for a time the seat of the court of the Emperor

Sigismund, was visited by the Emperor Frederick III, and maintained relations with the Aragonese court in Naples. There can be little doubt that in the aggregate these connections served not only to familiarise Sienese artists with Milanese and with French Gothic style, but to confine Sienese taste within limits as narrow as those of Milanese and Neapolitan court painting.

Like all court art, Sienese painting in the fifteenth century developed under an external stimulus and not under an impetus provided from within. There are few major altarpieces of the century which do not owe something to prototypes evolved in Florence. It is unlikely, for example, that Sassetta would have painted his *Madonna of the Snow* (Plates I-V), had the achievement of Masaccio not been in the forefront of his mind: without the precedent of Fra Angelico, Giovanni di Paolo's *Paradiso* (Plates XXVI-VII) would have assumed a very different form: Matteo di Giovanni would never have evolved his open-mouthed *St. Thomas* (Plate LIX), had it not been for paintings by the Pollajuoli: Francesco di Giorgio's *Madonna* at Amiens (Plate LXXVI) is based on a painting by Verrocchio: and the only artist in the entire century to remain immune from contacts of this kind, Sano di Pietro, rapidly atrophied for want of the sustenance of which his contemporaries availed themselves.

But great as was the debt of Sienese artists to Florentine painting, it was seldom that Florence exercised more than a superficial influence over painting in Siena. The rigid intellectual discipline of Florentine studios, their insistence on an almost mathematical coherence of design, their carefully inculcated lessons in geometry had no parallel in the training of Sienese artists, and for this reason Sienese painters as a whole tended to imitate specific Florentine paintings without endeavouring to emulate the methods which made these achievements possible.

At the same time the reluctance of Sienese artists to indoctrinate their pupils with the quasi-scientific formulae of Florentine studios left Sienese painting a loose and flexible medium for the expression of the painter's personality. Confronted by the daily problems of his trade, the Sienese painter offers solutions which are often unconventional and sometimes leave us with a sense of direct communion with the artist's mind. Where are we to find parallels for the central panel of Sassetta's polyptych at Cortona (Plate IX), for Giovanni di Paolo's *St. John entering the Wilderness* (Fig. 13), for Neroccio's *Annunciation* (Plates LXXXVIII-IX)? It is clear when we examine these paintings that if the nature of his training deprived the Sienese artist of certain advantages, it facilitated and indeed encouraged a type of formal improvisation, which has no equivalent elsewhere in Italian painting. This same absence of constraint lends many Sienese predella panels a spontaneity which gives them in their period a place akin to that of English water-colour painting in the nineteenth century. How seldom did painters in the quattrocento treat nature with the unforced, unaffected sympathy with which Giovanni di Paolo depicts the lilies, violets and carnations, the rabbits and the fruit-trees in his *Paradiso* (Plate XXVII). How seldom in the painting of the fifteenth century do we encounter the stormy sky and foaming sea of his *Miracle of St. Nicholas of Tolentino* (Frontispiece).

But the continuance in fifteenth century Siena of the technical processes and methods of the fourteenth century had a cause more fundamental than conservative distaste for artistic innovation, and we shall not understand the idiom of Sienese quattrocento painting unless we remember that, to a quite unusual degree, religious literature in fifteenth century Siena perpetuated what we may loosely call the mysticism of the fourteenth century. Whether it is St. Catherine of Siena (Fig. 2) who declares in the *Dialogo* that she is 'drunk with the light of faith', a late fourteenth century poet who describes himself as melting 'like wax before a fire' in the heat of divine love, or San Bernardino (Fig. 3) who apostrophises 'la più nobile Duchessa che fusse mai nell'universo; e la più nobile Reina, e la più nobile Imperadrice . . . coronata di dodici stelle . . . vestita d'oro e di sole', the note of mystical fervour remains the same. To this the hagiography of the Sienese mystics comes as a natural corollary. 'I shall say nothing', protests Addison in his

FIG. 2. *Vecchietta: St. Catherine of Siena (S. Catarina della Notte, Siena)*

Remarks on Several Parts of Italy, 'of the many gross and absurd traditions of St. Catherine of Sienna, who is the great Saint of this Place. I think there is as much pleasure in hearing a Man tell his Dreams as in reading accounts of this Nature.' Just as the rationalist tendency of Florentine religious thought is reflected in the representational urge of fifteenth century Florentine artists, so the mysticism of Siena is mirrored in the anti-realistic bias of Sienese quattrocento painting.

Here, too, we have an explanation of the emotional, often passionate, gestures of such figures as the Virgin in the *Crucifixion* of Matteo di Giovanni (Plate LXI), where the insistent pathos reflects with astonishing fidelity the trend of Sienese religious thought. The Sienese artist was no mystic and no saint. But all of the painters represented in this volume would have exclaimed with Richard Jefferies: 'I see nothing astonishing in what are called miracles. Only those who are mesmerised by matter can find a difficulty in such events', and so persuasive is the simple faith of Sano di Pietro's *Miracle of San Bernardino* (Fig. 4) that instinctively we look up at the sky in the hope that the figure of the Saint will emerge from the centre of some cloud to interrupt a funeral or intervene in a street accident. Whether founded on the rock of personal devotion (how else are we to explain the prayer 'Dominicus Domini Matrem Te Pinxit et Orat' below Domenico di Bartolo's *Madonna* of 1433 (Plate XXXVIII) or the phrase 'sui devotionis fecit hoc' beneath Vecchietta's *Risen Christ*?), or the expression of some collective appeal (how closely the inscription 'si confidis in me Sena eris gratia plena' in the halo of Sassetta's *Madonna of the Snow* (Plate III) recalls Sermini's apostrophe of the 'regina pur di vita eterna', whose holy mantle shields the city of Siena), a sense of the immanence of the supernatural colours the whole of Sienese quattrocento art.

Nowhere do these qualities receive more unequivocal expression than in the work of the first of the painters represented in this book. Born about 1400, perhaps at Cortona, whence his parents migrated to Siena, Sassetta appears to have been trained in the studio of one of the many artists who preserved into the fifteenth century the heavy, precedent-ridden style of the last years of the trecento. But from the first his work was stamped by a more intimate, more intellectual attitude to painting than that of artists of an earlier generation, and by 1432, when he completed the earliest of his extant altarpieces, a *Madonna of the Snow* for the Sienese Duomo (Plates I-V), few traces of the lessons he had learned during his youth remained. In the form of the picture, with its vigorous definition of the four planes on which the kneeling saints, the Virgin and the standing saints, the standing angels, and the angels protruding above the throne, are placed, we can find evidence of Sassetta's

FIG. 3. *Neroccio: S. Bernardino preaching in the Piazza del Campo (Palazzo Pubblico, Siena)*

(10)

FIG. 4. *Sano di Pietro: S. Bernardino resuscitates a dead Child (Lady Catherine Ashburnham, Ashburnham)*

study of the paintings of his Florentine contemporaries, and particularly of Masaccio, who on his death in 1428 had left unfinished in the Florentine priory of the Carmine the most advanced fresco cycle of his day. It is with the paintings of the most prominent of Masaccio's followers, the young Filippo Lippi, that Sassetta's *Madonna* shows its closest points of contact, and for certain features of the painting—the pose of the foreshortened angels above the throne (Plate III) and the retracted lips and enigmatic smile of the figure to its left—we can find precedents in Lippi's early works. But Florentine painting provides no precedent for the emotional tension of the altarpiece, and we can guess that the resentment with which the authorities of the Sienese Cathedral seem to have greeted Sassetta's audacious composition, would have been mitigated by the decorative splendour of the painting, by the inspired figures of the Baptist (Plate II) and St. Francis (Plate IV), and by the entrancing profile of the fair-haired angel kneading a ball of snow (Plate V).

For Sassetta the form of the *Madonna of the Snow* was to remain an exception rather than the rule, and during the 1430's his paintings reverted to a style in which the creation of a three-dimensional illusion was sacrificed to linear design. Symptomatic of this tendency is a polyptych painted for Cortona about 1434 (Plates IX-XII). In this two angels seated in the left foreground and right background of the central panel (Plate XII) lend the Virgin and Child, one of the most beautiful groups in fifteenth century Italian painting (Plate X), something of the character of free-standing statuary. But the lateral saints (Plate XI) are once again the isolated figures of a Gothic polyptych, a group of self-consistent units without the emotional or visual unity of the earlier altarpiece. Some indication of the reasons for this change is afforded about 1436 by the seven *Scenes from the Life of St. Anthony the Abbot,* where for the first time we can detect the influence of French book illumination. As in a miniature, the inverted S formed by the path in the *Meeting of St. Anthony the Abbot and St. Paul the Hermit* (Plate VI), the birds strung out above the convex line of the horizon in the *Temptation of St. Anthony* (Plate VIII), and the writhing tree trunks of the

Scourging of St. Anthony (Plate VII), establish a unity of rhythm which elevates each scene above the plane of day-to-day experience and carries it to a remote, imaginary world.

It would be wrong, however, to suggest that the interest of the *Scenes from the Life of St. Anthony* depends upon calligraphy alone, for in the eloquent left hand with which the Saint repels his temptress, and the embracing figures of Saints Anthony and Paul outside the hermit's cell, Sassetta shows himself an illustrator of exquisite and often penetrating subtlety. In a sequence of *Scenes from the Life of St. Francis* (Plates XIII-XIX), completed for the church of S. Francesco at Borgo San Sepolcro in 1444, the full scope of Sassetta's genius for narrative reveals itself. The series of eight panels opens with the twin episodes of *St. Francis dreaming of the Celestial City* (Plate XIV), visualised in the imagery of Bonaventure as 'quel palagio tutto pieno d'armi di croce tutte dipinte e segnate della croce di Cristo', and the *Charity of St. Francis* (Plate XV), as it had been recorded by the Saint's biographer, Thomas of Celano, and culminates in the *Funeral of St. Francis* (Plate XVI), in which a look of inexpressible anguish crosses the faces of his followers as the knight Jerome, who had doubted the miracle of the Stigmata, bends down to place his hand in the wound in the Saint's side and Madonna Jacopa da Settensoli, kneeling before the bier, bathes the Saint's body in her tears. Last and most lovely of the scenes is the *Mystic Marriage of St. Francis* (Plate XVII). It was Bonaventure who described how St. Francis, journeying with a companion towards Siena, encountered the visionary figures of Chastity, Obedience and Poverty, but it was Sassetta who determined to set the scene before the outline of Monte Amiata and the patterned fields of the Sienese *contado,* who visualised the Saint plighting his troth with Poverty (Plate XIX) and who depicted the three Virtues flying heavenward as Poverty looks back towards her spouse. In the frescoes at Assisi we see episodes from St. Francis' life as they were conceived by members of the generation following his own; Sassetta's panels show us the Franciscan legend of the fifteenth century, embroidered by the artifice of countless literary narratives, illuminated by the fervour of San Bernardino and his companions at the Osservanza, and interpreted by one of the consummate visual artists of his day.

In the early paintings of Sassetta's contemporary, Giovanni di Paolo, we find reflections of Sassetta's style. It is reasonably certain, for example, that the central figure of the *Madonna and Child in a Landscape* in the Boston Museum of Fine Arts (Plate XXII), painted about 1436, was based on a *Madonna* by Sassetta, and that the distant landscape and the curved line of the wood (Plate XXIV) owe something to the influences which inspired Sassetta's *Temptation of St. Anthony.* But in all other respects Giovanni di Paolo's artistic personality stands in sharp contrast to Sassetta's. The interest in formal relationships, which distinguishes Sassetta's work, evoked no echo in the younger painter's mind, and when we compare the Boston *Madonna* with the late *Madonna* by Sassetta in the Frick collection (Plate XX), we find the linear rhythm of Sassetta's prototype disrupted by a multiplicity of naturalistic details and the cold, almost sculptural figures of the Virgin and the Child restated in more animated and more human terms (Plate XXIII). No less striking are the differences between Giovanni di Paolo's predella panel of the *Paradiso* in the Metropolitan Museum, New York (Plates XXVI-VII), probably painted in 1445, and Sassetta's *Scenes from the Life of St. Francis.* In place of the careful spacing of Sassetta's panels, we find a crowded composition, where the eye is constantly caught up by details, incidental to the main theme of the painting. Oblivious to the principle of visual unity by which Sassetta's panels were inspired, Giovanni di Paolo is the exponent of a more diffuse, colloquial and impulsive narrative technique. But if for a moment we erase the memory of Sassetta from our minds, how fascinating the two scenes become. The innocent sentiment of the *Madonna,* seated on her brocaded cushion amid a flower strewn field, the rapture of the men and women who encounter one another in the fields of Paradise, the lilies and ranunculus which spring up beside them and the rabbits which play round their feet, admit us to the intimacy of an artist whose determination to express the emotional quintessence of each scene was to induce a sometimes callous disrespect for the aesthetic preconceptions of his day.

The spirit in which Giovanni di Paolo interpreted the Dantesque imagery of the *Paradiso* comes to full fruition in a miniature of the *Triumph of Death* (Plate XXV), from an antiphonal which seems to date from shortly after 1450. In this moving scene the familiar mediaeval theme is transported to the realm of personal experience, as humanity, personified by a solitary man standing before a wood, face lined with apprehension at his impending destiny and hands clasped in prayer, is overtaken by a menacing winged figure girded with a scythe, who gallops through the centre of the scene on a cadaverous black horse.

With an almost contemporary panel of *St. Nicholas of Tolentino saving a Ship at Sea* (Frontispiece) the change foretold in the *Triumph of Death* is complete. Just as Sassetta in the *Scenes from the Life of St. Anthony the Abbot* evolved an idiom which gave his panels a new imaginative life, so Giovanni di Paolo after 1450 moved gradually towards a style which existed on its own imaginative plane unfettered by logic or fact. When Addison compared the mysticism of St. Catherine of Siena to the narration of dreams, it was no doubt the part played by the subconscious in forming the visions of the mystic and the dreamer that to his eyes vitiated both types of experience. But for a generation which no longer shares this formal prejudice, few experiences in Italian painting are more exciting than to follow Giovanni di Paolo as he plunges, like Alice, through the looking-glass which separates reality from super-realism to explore the resources of a mystical, and therefore of a partially subconscious, world.

From the kneeling sailors who appeal to St. Nicholas of Tolentino as their storm-tossed vessel, its mast and sails blowing against the lowering sky, rides through the deep green sea, we may turn at once to Giovanni di Paolo's masterpiece, two interrelated cycles of *Scenes from the Life of St. John Baptist* in the Art Institute of Chicago (Plates XXVIII-XXX) and the National Gallery in London (Plates XXXI-IV). Of the first of these cycles, a set of twelve scenes designed to form the wings of an altarpiece or shrine (perhaps containing a single figure of St. John like the horrifying monolith of *St. Jerome* (Plate XXXV) in the Museo dell'Opera del Duomo at Siena), ten panels are preserved. Of the second and later cycle, a set of five predella panels, four scenes survive. Two scenes are repeated with relatively little variation in both sets of panels, and it is in these that Giovanni di Paolo's aspirations are most fully realised. In the first scene *St. John Baptist entering the Wilderness* (Plates XXXIII-IV, Fig. 13) we see the youthful Baptist twice, once with a staff over his shoulder leaving the city gate and a second time climbing a hilly path with steps so light that his red-stockinged feet seem to fly over the ground. To right and left are jagged crags and a precipitous ravine, while in the foreground, as from an eminence, we look down on patterned fields, intersected by white roads. Unlike Sassetta's St. Anthony the Abbot, whose stature diminishes in the ratio of the distance at which he is portrayed, Giovanni di Paolo's St. John retains the same dimensions in the middle distance as in the foreground of the scene, while the trees which break up the landscape on the right decrease in size as they approach the forefront of the picture space. In the panel of the *Meeting of St. John with Christ* (Plate XXVIII), the irrational character of this deeply original conception is enhanced by a flat distance treated like a map and by a landscape (Plate XXX) which puts to new and unexpectedly fantastic use the system of geometrical progression invented in the 1430's by Uccello and the Florentine perspectivists. The formal interest of the second scene, *The Presentation of the Baptist's Head to Herod* (Fig. 14), is not comparable to that of *St. John entering the Wilderness*. But here the same dramatic instinct which enables us to share in the young Baptist's pilgrimage takes on an unexampled narrative intensity, as Herod lifts his hands in horror at the Baptist's severed head, and Salome, with an emphasis which would be less surprising in Wilde or Strauss than in a fifteenth century religious artist, places the veil which she has taken from the charger on the table and gathering up her train begins to dance.

Of the many imitators of Sassetta's style, relatively few emerged as artistic personalities in their own

FIG. 5. *Studio of Jacopo della Quercia: Madonna (S. Martino, Siena)*

right. The most individual of these, Pietro di Giovanni d'Ambrogio, painted in 1444 a processional banner, now in the Musée Jacquemart André in Paris, on one side of which we see a figure of *St. Catherine in Glory* (Fig. 11-12 and Plate XXI) (evidently connected with the central panel of Sassetta's altarpiece for Borgo San Sepolcro), while on the reverse is a representation of the *Crucifixion,* which has something of the monumentality of Sassetta's larger paintings. But it was through the work of a more celebrated and more prolific artist, Sano di Pietro, that the influence of Sassetta's style was transmitted to the painters of the later quattrocento. In his own day Sano di Pietro was the head of what may well have been the largest bottega in Siena, and in the eyes of posterity his reputation has suffered from the vast number of stereotyped *Madonnas* and polyptychs which pass under his name. It cannot be denied that beside the work of Giovanni di Paolo Sano's painting appears tepid, and beside that of Sassetta crude. But autograph examples of his work, of which a *Madonna and Child* in the Osservanza at Siena is representative (Plate XXXVII), do something to redress the balance, and afford a glimpse of the authentic individuality of a not insensitive artist. Moreover, the vast majority of Sano di Pietro's altarpieces were designed to satisfy the unexacting demands of local churches in the villages around Siena, and his smaller panels (Plate XXXVI) show a simplicity of form and narrative technique, which sometimes reminds us of the Douanier Rousseau and affords a useful guide to popular taste in the middle of the fifteenth century.

Some of Sano di Pietro's most distinguished work was produced during the later 1440's under the influence of Domenico di Bartolo, an artist whose eclectic temperament and advanced aesthetic principles had few points in common with his own. The rapid development of representational painting in Florence in the first half of the quattrocento is due largely to the interaction of pictorial and sculptural styles. Interested primarily in the depiction of volume and the accurate rendering of natural appearances, Domenico di Bartolo was the only Sienese painter of his day seriously to concern himself with the problem of investing two-dimensional paintings with the properties of sculpture in the round. How far this should be attributed to Domenico's familiarity with Florentine artists and Florentine bottegas and how far it should be referred to the close contacts he enjoyed with Jacopo della Quercia, the great Sienese sculptor of the first half of the fifteenth century, it is difficult to say. But his earliest surviving work, a *Madonna and Child with six Angels* of 1433 in the Siena Gallery (Plate XXXVIII), leaves little doubt that both these factors exercised some influence on his style, for the heads of the figures remind us of Alberti's advocacy of 'painting which has deep relief and appears to the spectator very similar to the bodies which it represents', while their drapery recalls the shallow recesses of Jacopo della Quercia's statuary (Fig. 5). The *Madonna* of 1433 is not only Domenico's earliest, but also his most mellow and attractive work, and by 1437, the date of a *Madonna and Child before a Hedge of Roses* in the Johnson Collection at Philadelphia (Plate XXXIX), he had developed a more forbidding and more monumental style. In this painting indeed the scheme is not unlike that of Florentine marble reliefs of the second quarter of the century, the two figures filling a larger proportion of the picture space than in any other Sienese *Madonna* of comparable dimensions and the Child being invested with a sense of weight which has no sanction in Sienese quattrocento art.

A monumental style requires a monumental field, and it is no coincidence that Domenico di Bartolo should have been responsible between 1441 and 1444 for painting in the Pellegrinaio of the Spedale della Scala the most important fresco cycle executed in Siena during the fifteenth century. Designed to illustrate the history and day-to-day activities of the Hospital, the cycle shows the rector of the Hospital receiving privileges from Pope Celestine III, the enlargement of the Hospital, the reception of the sick in the Pellegrinaio, the distribution of whole loaves of bread, which took place weekly outside the precincts of the Hospital (Fig. 16), and last and most curious the nurture, education and marriage of the foundlings for whose upbringing the Hospital authorities assumed responsibility (Fig. 15). To the then rector of the Hospital, who was certainly familiar with the frescoes painted in analogous Florentine institutions, Domenico di Bartolo's style, with its superficial Florentinism, would have been specially congenial, while the contemporary character of certain of the scenes called for the naturalistic treatment which alone of Sienese artists Domenico was able to supply. But a cycle of such dimensions demanded greater genius than Domenico di Bartolo's, and with the exception of the fresco representing the *Feeding of the Poor,* the scenes reveal a fundamental structural weakness very different from that of the Florentine prototypes from which they derive. Indeed it is tempting to suppose that when Alberti in his treatise on painting condemned artists who 'in order to induce an effect of

FIG. 6. *Vecchietta: Madonna and Child with SS. John Baptist and Catherine of Alexandria (Kaiser Friedrich Museum, Berlin)*

richness and because of their reluctance to leave any part of their picture unfilled, fail to subordinate their work to any scheme of composition and spread the elements of their paintings about in confusion', he had such a fresco as Domenico di Bartolo's *Marriage of the Foundlings* in mind. Today, therefore, the fascination of the frescoes rests less in the completed works than in the treatment of isolated figures, the grimacing woman who is interrupted at her task of warming linen by the fire (Plate XL), the nurse who caresses the grotesque child standing on her knee, the impassive hospital official who commits one of the foundlings to its foster-mother (Plate XLI), or the woman waiting with her children to receive alms from the Hospital (Plate XLIII), where we can sense in all its freshness the bewilderment with which the early naturalists reacted to the mystery of gesture and the enigma of the human countenance.

Though Domenico di Bartolo was responsible for the bulk of the frescoes in the Pellegrinaio, the scheme of decoration seems to have been initiated not by Domenico but by an artist who was to exercise profound influence on the painters of the later quattrocento, Lorenzo Vecchietta. Vecchietta appears to have been trained under Sassetta, from whom he inherited his firm sense of design. It is Sassetta's style, for example, that conditions the earliest of his paintings, a small *Madonna* in the Kaiser Friedrich Museum in Berlin (Fig. 6). By 1441, however, when he completed a fresco of *The Foundation of the Hospital* in the Pellegrinaio, he had come under the influence of Domenico Veneziano and contemporary Florentine painting, and though it evinces greater decorative sense and a stronger feeling for pictorial structure than the adjacent frescoes of Domenico di Bartolo, it is conceived in the same naturalistic terms. But where naturalism was the be-all and the end-all of Domenico di Bartolo's style, in Vecchietta it was redeemed by a narrative talent second to none in Sienese painting. His narrative gift can be seen at its best in an illuminated codex of the *Divine Comedy* in the British Museum, in which his own miniatures to the *Inferno* and the *Purgatorio* were completed by a set of illustrations to the *Paradiso* by Giovanni di Paolo. It is from this book that the illustrations of *The Wood of the Suicides* (Plate XLV) and of *The Earthly Paradise* (Plate XLVI), with its enchanting image of Dante overcome by sleep (Plate XLVII) and its representation of the poet's magical greeting to Matilda:

> *Tu mi fai rimembrar dove e qual era*
> *Proserpina nel tempo che perdette*
> *la madre lei, ed ella primavera,*

in the present volume derive. We meet the tense, muscular figures of the *Wood of the Suicides* and the placid landscape of the *Earthly Paradise* again in the cycle of the frescoes which Vecchietta executed three or four years later in the sacristy of the church of S. Maria della Scala. But the frescoes themselves are much damaged, and it is only the disarming innocence of Vecchietta's Adam and Eve that affords a just impression of what was perhaps the most accomplished wall decoration produced in Siena in the fifteenth century.

Between 1448, when the frescoes in the sacristy were completed, and 1450, the date of the commencement of a cycle of frescoes in the Baptistry of San Giovanni, a change comes over Vecchietta's style. Indeed in the scenes of *The Flagellation* and *Christ carrying the Cross* we find in the brutal, grimacing faces a tendency towards expressionism not unlike that which we have noted in Giovanni di Paolo's work of about the same time. But the figures are grotesque rather than moving, and the scenes as a whole mark an aberration and not an advance in Vecchietta's career. By the close of the 1450's, however, the artist reverts to a more monumental style (Plate XLVIII), and when in 1461 he executes his most personal and successful work, the full-length figure of St. Catherine of Siena emerging from a painted niche in the Sienese Palazzo Pubblico (Plate XLIV), it is clear that the treatment is deliberately sculptural in character. In the last decades of his life Vecchietta was in fact engaged on large-scale bronzes, and it is not altogether surprising that during this period even the standing saints in the wings of his polyptychs (Plate XLIX) should take on the rugged, uncompromising character of works cast in bronze.

It was in the studio of Vecchietta that Matteo di Giovanni, the artist whose personality dominates Sienese painting during the second half of the fifteenth century, was trained. Born in or shortly before 1435, Matteo inherited the naturalistic aspirations of Vecchietta, and we find the rigid, sculptural forms of Vecchietta's larger paintings reflected in his early works. But where Vecchietta's paintings and frescoes evince a disrespect for medium not altogether unexpected in an artist whose main interest was in sculpture, it needs no more than the raised pigment and the summary, expressionistic forms of a predella panel of the *Crucifixion* (Plate LXI) from an altarpiece painted before 1460 for the church of S. Agostino at Asciano to demonstrate that Matteo di Giovanni was a painter born.

Matteo di Giovanni's father was a native of Borgo San Sepolcro, and it is likely that Matteo himself retained much the same contacts with Borgo San Sepolcro as Sassetta with the neighbouring township of Cortona in the first half of the century. These contacts are no doubt accountable for the fact that about 1465 Matteo was invited to Borgo San Sepolcro to complete the lateral and subsidiary panels of the altarpiece of *The Baptism of Christ,* which Piero della Francesca had designed a quarter of a century before for the Priory of San Giovanni. Of the anomalies of the commission, this is no place to speak. But there can be no doubt that incongruous as was the setting in which Matteo placed the *Baptism* and scant as were his sympathies for Piero's original intentions, the commission served to introduce him to one of the great painters of the fifteenth century. The delayed impact of an artist's work is sometimes greater than the direct influence of his personality, and in the case of Matteo di Giovanni it was the solid architectural scheme and monumental forms of the *Baptism of Christ* which developed what had been a provincial talent along broader lines, and memories of the pearly lights in which Piero della Francesca's figures are suffused and of the sense of isolation and detachment which they communicate that inspired his masterpiece, the *Madonna and Child with two Angels* in the Pieve at Buonconvento (Plate LIV).

Between 1470, the putative date of the Buonconvento *Madonna,* and 1475, the year in which Matteo di Giovanni seems to have completed the altarpiece of the *Assumption of the Virgin* in the National Gallery (Plate LVI), other influences supervened on Piero's. In the *Assumption* the system of large-scale organisation, which Matteo di Giovanni learned from Piero, survives, while the landscape (so reminiscent of the dry, generalised terms in which Biondo Flavio in an almost contemporary diary describes the country round Asciano) is closely related to the landscape behind the *Baptism*. But when we examine the detailed treatment of the painting, we encounter the style of the Florentine naturalists of the generation following Piero's, and particularly of Antonio del Pollajuolo, whose altarpiece of *The Martyrdom of St. Sebastian* in the National Gallery, completed in 1475 for the Florentine Church of S. Sebastiano, provides a point of reference for the *Assumption*. In particular the bronzed, open-mouthed St. Thomas (Plate LXI), silhouetted against the panoramic landscape, is redolent of the Pollajuolo school. But where the archers in the foreground of the Pollajuolo *Martyrdom of St. Sebastian* are depicted as solid figures, Matteo di Giovanni's St. Thomas is a figure in limited relief within an outline drawn on a single plane. So alien to Florentine naturalistic painting, this insistence on the linear basis of pictorial forms is still more evident in the Christ and prophets in the upper section of the altarpiece (Plate LX), and here it is very probable that the forms were suggested to Matteo di Giovanni by the miniatures of Girolamo da Cremona, who between 1468 and 1475 was engaged in decorating the choir-books of the Duomo at Siena in a style which adapted the Northern classicism of Mantegna to the linear requirements of book illumination.

It would be wrong, however, to suggest that Matteo di Giovanni's style was conditioned solely by these classicistic influences to the exclusion of the authentic classical sources from which the style of the Pollajuoli in Florence or of Mantegna in North Italy derived. Indeed, from 1475 on the story of Matteo di Giovanni's development is that of a sustained endeavour to assimilate antiquity. Since the seventeenth century the classical current in European painting has been bound up with a reaction against realism. But in the quattrocento not only was assimilation of antiquity not inconsistent with the growth of realism, but it proceeded hand in hand with the development of a naturalistic style. It is thus no accident that the more classical Matteo di Giovanni's style becomes, the more pronounced become its naturalistic tendencies. The implications of this development may most readily be gauged in a pavement of

FIG. 7. *Matteo di Giovanni: The Massacre of the Innocents (Duomo, Siena)*

The Massacre of the Innocents (Fig. 7), designed in 1481 for the floor of the Sienese Cathedral, and in an altarpiece of the same subject completed in the following year for the church of S. Agostino in Siena (Plate LXII). The earlier scheme is a flat, frieze-like composition, of the type of which Botticelli's rather later *Calumny* is a familiar example. A classical relief in the entablature above the columns provides the keynote for the treatment and even for the poses of the women and soldiers shown below, while from an aperture pierced above each arch there leans out a group of children manifesting unconcealed enjoyment at the carnage carried out beneath them. The altarpiece of 1482 makes use of a more concentrated scheme, but it retains the antique colonnade and the sadistic children of the earlier composition, while the grimacing masks of the women and the contorted features of the executioners (Plates LXIII-V) generate a sometimes horrible intensity.

Had Matteo di Giovanni pursued the uncompromising realism of this painting, we cannot tell where it might not have led him. But in the last two decades of the century the intellectual climate of Siena was not one to encourage enterprise or innovation, and it is to the enervating influence of an increasingly autocratic system that we must ascribe the reversion of Matteo di Giovanni towards 1490 to a tamer and more formal style. A *Madonna and Child with two Saints* in the Barber Institute at Birmingham (Plate LV) shows us the final evolution of Matteo's work towards a flat pattern, in which the normal spatial relationship between the figures is abandoned in favour of a purely decorative scheme and the delicate modelling of the heads is indicated in what is in effect a magnified silverpoint technique beneath the glazes of the highly worked surface of the panel.

We may pass rapidly over the work of Guidoccio Cozzarelli, a pupil and imitator of Matteo di Giovanni, and of Benvenuto di Giovanni. Cozzarelli's smaller works betray an engaging garrulity, which is a not unpleasant contrast to the rather taciturn temperament of Matteo. Moreover, unlike Matteo di Giovanni, he enjoyed a considerable practice as a book illuminator (Fig. 8), and did not hesitate to introduce the gay and sometimes unconventional methods of book illumination into his predella panels. Who, for example, would guess at first sight that Cozzarelli's enchantingly informal *Annunciation and Flight into Egypt* in the National Gallery at Washington (Plates LXVI-VIII) was a panel painting and not a miniature? With Benvenuto di Giovanni we come upon a painter with a more distinct artistic personality. A year younger than Matteo, Benvenuto di Giovanni was trained in the Vecchietta studio. But though his

style till middle life retained a morphological connection with Vecchietta's (the incisive outline of the
lateral saints in the *Madonna and Child with SS. Peter
and Nicholas of Bari* of 1479 in the National Gallery in
London (Fig. 18), for example, depends directly on
Vecchietta), he had as little natural sympathy with
the grim realism of Vecchietta as with the slow cere-
bration of Matteo di Giovanni. It is perhaps to Benvenuto di Giovanni at a time when he was employed
in Vecchietta's shop that we owe a panel of *The
Preaching of S. Bernardino* in the Walker Art Gallery
at Liverpool (Fig. 17). With its deficiency in dramatic emphasis (the figure of the preaching Saint
(Plate LXX) is reduced to the dimensions of an
architectural ornament on the façade behind the
scene), its flimsy, decorative buildings, and its slight,
doll-like figures, it forms a fit opening to the work
of a painter whose career was dogged by the desire
to please. And please Benvenuto di Giovanni does,

FIG. 8. *Guidoccio Cozzarelli: Ecce Agnus Dei (Private Collection)*

for if ease of manner, unfaltering taste, and a carefully cultivated naivete were the hallmarks of success,
the flat pattern and the simple forms of the *Adoration of the Magi* (Plate LXIX), and the coy smile of
the flower-decked angel (Plate LXXII) who peers over the throne in the National Gallery *Madonna*,
would rank with the great achievements of Sienese painting.

If Benvenuto di Giovanni was the Romney of the quattrocento, Francesco di Giorgio Martini was its
Reynolds. A painter, sculptor, archaeologist, engineer, architect and writer, Francesco is the type of the
humane and versatile court artist of the later fifteenth century. Employed by Federigo da Montefeltro at
Urbino and by the Duke of Calabria at Naples, invited to Milan to work on designs for the Cathedral, he
built up a career which in some respects ran parallel to that of Leonardo. But though Francesco di
Giorgio was Leonardo's senior only by twelve or thirteen years, his mental make-up was that of the
generation before Leonardo's. Devoid of Leonardo's interest in natural forms, of Leonardo's scientific
curiosity and intellectual empiricism, Francesco di Giorgio's was a less complicated and less formidable
personality.

During his lifetime Francesco di Giorgio was regarded as an architect and sculptor rather than as a
painter, and of the sixty lines of a poetic eulogy prepared in 1490 by Giovanni Santi only one refers to his
pictorial work. What Francesco di Giorgio was for his contemporaries he remains today, and the phrase
'presto, veloce, et alto depintore', with which Giovanni Santi sums up his achievement, epitomises the
main features of Francesco's style. While his paintings do not attain the transcendent quality of his reliefs
and while for the most part they date from a relatively early phase in his career, they have at their best a
spontaneity which ensures them a place apart in quattrocento painting. Whether this is due, as Giovanni
Santi's line suggests, to the speed at which Francesco worked, or whether it was some more personal
quality which enabled him to preserve in the completed work the freshness of his first inspiration, we
cannot tell, but the fact remains that he was master of a peculiar effervescent gaiety, which gives his lay
decorations the chic of a quattrocento Marie Laurencin and lends his small religious paintings a special
tenderness and charm.

Francesco di Giorgio's earliest surviving painting, a panel of *St. Dorothy* in the National Gallery in

London (Plate LXXIII), belongs to a moment when Francesco had emerged from, and was still impregnated with the spirit of, the Vecchietta studio. Childlike in its simplicity—the scheme derives from a contemporary South German woodcut—the little painting, with its chalky colouring and consciously unrealistic setting, speaks the same language as Benvenuto di Giovanni's early *Preaching of S. Bernardino*. But the sharp folds of the drapery betray Francesco's awakening interest in sculpture and anticipate the more incisive qualities of his mature work. It is in a rather later panel of the *Nativity* in the collection of Sir Frederick Cook (Plate LXXVII), however, painted probably *ca.* 1465 when Francesco had come into contact with the Florentine altarpieces of Fra Filippo Lippi and with the miniatures of Girolamo da Cremona, that we encounter the true beauties of his early style. Built up of pigment which seems blown rather than brushed on to the surface of the panel, the figures of the Virgin, bending with parted lips over the stiff and unresponsive Child, and of St. Joseph, his weary head supported on his hand, are conceived with the intimacy of a casual sketch. Still more enchanting is a small *Annunciation* of about 1470 in the Siena Gallery (Plate LXXV), in which the Virgin, sitting at a fantastic lectern before a double colonnade, is confronted by an angel so radiant as to seem a true visitant from another world. Both the Cook *Nativity* and the *Annunciation* in Siena make use of realistic elements from the paintings of Francesco's Florentine contemporaries. But especially in the latter painting the preposterous architecture, with its obstinate neglect of what for Francesco di Giorgio as for Geoffrey Scott was 'the mechanical bondage of construction', the false perspective of the lectern and the angel's unsteady stance are tantamount to a protest at the prosaic methods and the sometimes heavy footed pedantry of Florentine quattrocento painting.

In Francesco di Giorgio's larger altarpieces some of the qualities of these small paintings are preserved, but whether in the *Holy Family* of 1475 in the Siena Gallery (Plate LXXIV) or in the later and drier *Adoration of the Shepherds* in S. Domenico, we cannot but be conscious that their spontaneity is won at the expense of structural unity. Indeed at first sight it appears that these strange, enigmatic paintings are in the nature of rapidly expanded sketches rather than of the carefully evolved designs which would normally have been regarded as appropriate to a formal altarpiece. Be this as it may, it is only in one relatively late painting, a *Madonna and Child* in the Musée de Picardie at Amiens (Plate LXXVI), in which the motifs of the parapet behind the figure, the river estuary seen through the window, the hard drapery and the sharp knuckles of the hands are based on pictures by Verrocchio, that Francesco di Giorgio escapes from the metaphysical extravagance which marks his later style.

Giovanni Santi describes the zeal with which Francesco di Giorgio preserved and studied the ruins of classical temples, and Francesco's secular paintings reveal one and all the romantic nostalgia for antiquity so typical of the Renaissance mind. The artist's *taccuini* testify to the scope of his classical studies, but it is to his cassone panels, with their limpid handling and ready incident, that we must turn if we are to become familiar with an interpretative talent which could distil the magic of classical mythology with a touch scarcely less confident than Piero di Cosimo's in the *Forest Fire* or Raphael's in the *Vision of a Knight*. What Piero di Cosimo could do for Lucretius and Raphael for Silius Italicus, Francesco does for the *Metamorphoses* in a panel of the *Rape of Europa* in the Louvre (Fig. 9), where on the right we see Europa timidly mounting the back of the white bull, whose horns she has decorated with a wreath of flowers, and on the left the frightened girl, her skirt billowing in the breeze, borne by what Dolce not inaptly termed 'l'astuto toro' towards the sea. Considerably later than this panel, a drawing of *Atlas* at Brunswick (Plate LXXVIII) shows us the standing figure of the Titan, his arms tense under the weight which heaven with all its stars presses upon him, and his right leg erect above the axis of the world which he rotates with his free foot. What more arresting treatment of a figure from mythology is to be found in the whole fifteenth century?

Almost contemporary with this drawing and certainly painted after 1485 is a small panel in the Metro-

FIG. 9. *Francesco di Giorgio: The Rape of Europa (Louvre, Paris)*

politan Museum (Plate LXXX-I), which perhaps illustrates the scene from *Huon of Bordeaux* where the fate of the two lovers round whom the story centres is determined by the outcome of a game of chess. Whatever the subject, the intent youth seated by the table, the casual spectators and the girl who raises her eyes longingly from the board (Plate LXXXI), exhale the atmosphere of the quattrocento *novellieri* and of the elegant imitations of Boccaccio, with which prosperous houses in Siena would have been regaled. The *Game of Chess* no doubt formed part of the external decoration of a chest. The fresco of *Fidelity* in the Mogmar Art Foundation (Plates LXXIX, Fig. 20), on the other hand, is the sole surviving fragment of what may well have been a painted room. In its conception the figure is not unlike the wood inlaid intarsias, with which Francesco is supposed to have adorned the Palace at Urbino, and it has many of the qualities—the frivolity, the facile prettiness, the rather superficial charm—which we associate with modern interior decoration.

Between 1469 and 1475 Francesco di Giorgio worked in partnership with a still younger member of the Vecchietta studio, Neroccio dei Landi. A greater and more individual painter than Francesco di Giorgio, it was inevitable that Neroccio's early work should reflect the influence of Francesco's. But despite the interaction of the artists upon one another during their half decade of collaboration, their personalities remain distinct. In Francesco we have an artist whose reputation extended through the length and breadth of Italy; in Neroccio a painter who worked solely in Siena. Francesco was a sculptor and engineer who turned out a relatively small number of pictures; Neroccio was an artist, who, apart from a few statues and reliefs, canalised his energies exclusively in painting. Francesco's paintings were personal, clever and uncertain; Neroccio's perfectly developed talent produced some of the most sensitive and best articulated paintings of the entire Sienese school.

The fact that Neroccio shared a studio with Francesco di Giorgio has given rise to the belief that the two artists were jointly responsible for executing certain paintings, and as a result many authentic early paintings by Neroccio have been attributed to Neroccio and Francesco di Giorgio working in collaboration. It may well be that according to the practice of the studio large commissions were distributed between Francesco and Neroccio, and that Neroccio's predella panels, for example, were designed to fit beneath Francesco's altarpieces. But there is no valid reason to believe that any extant panel is the joint product of both artists. Among the earliest of the paintings executed by Neroccio during the period of partnership must be a cassone panel of *Anthony and Cleopatra* in the National Gallery at Washington (Plates LXXXV, Fig. 19), which follows closely Plutarch's account of the arrival of the barge of Cleopatra in the River Cydnus:

> 'She herself lay all alone under a canopy of cloth of gold, dressed as Venus in a picture, and
> beautiful young boys, like painted Cupids, stood on each side to fan her. Her maids were dressed

like sea nymphs and graces, some steering at the rudder, some working at the ropes. The perfumes diffused themselves from the vessel to the shore, which was covered with multitudes, part following the galley up on either bank, part running out of the city to see the sight, while the word went through all the multitude that Venus was come to feast with Bacchus, for the common good of Asia.'

We meet the same playful and essentially literary attitude to the antique in the classical reliefs which form the background to a lunette of the *Annunciation* (Plate LXXXVIII-IX), painted soon after 1470 and now in the Gallery of Fine Arts at Yale University, where the elegant, spare figures seem to move in response to the taut rhythms of *Pulcinella* or *Apollo Musagetes*. The sense that the gods are indeed going begging is enhanced by the silhouette of the Virgin in the foreground, which is resolved in a pose derived from Simone Martini's *Annunciation* of 1333 in the Sienese Duomo. How different is the sentiment of such a painting from the sophisticated classicism of Francesco di Giorgio!

Painted not long after the *Annunciation* and certainly before 1475, a predella with *Scenes from the Life of St. Benedict* in the Uffizi (Plate LXXXIV) marks the turning point in Neroccio's career. Against a landscape background which recalls the simple landscape of the *Anthony and Cleopatra,* the band of youths attending upon Totila, with their lithe limbs and curling golden hair, affords a foretaste of the mandarin subtleties which, with the indefatigable idleness of a Chinese toymaker, Neroccio was to propagate for the next twenty years.

It is a moot point how far the character of any style is determined by the artist's predilections and how far it is decided by the predilections of clients whom he paints to please. Were it not the most captivating portrait of the fifteenth century, the *Portrait of a Girl* in the National Gallery at Washington (Plate LXXXVII), which Neroccio must have completed about 1480, would have an interest of its own as depicting the patron for whom such a painting as the *Anthony and Cleopatra* may well have been designed. Before the smooth complexion, the long, soft neck, the carefully dressed hair, the pencilled eyebrows of Neroccio's sitter, we are irresistibly reminded of Aeneas Sylvius' description of Lucretia, the heroine of *The Tale of the Two Lovers,* which was itself set in the Siena of 1444:

> 'Her hair was long, the colour of beaten gold . . . Her lofty forehead of good proportions was without a wrinkle, and her arched eyebrows were dark and slender with a due space between. Such was the splendour of her eyes that like the sun they dazzled all who looked on them; with such eyes she could kill whom she chose and, when she would, restore the dead to life. Her nose was straight in contour evenly dividing her rosy cheeks . . . . A small and well shaped mouth, coral lips made to be bitten, straight little teeth that shone like crystal, and between them running to and fro a tremulous tongue that uttered not speech but the sweetest harmonies . . . I think Helen was not more fair on that day when Menelaus received Paris at his feast, nor was Andromache more richly adorned when joined in holy wedlock with Hector.'

In the elegant periods of Aeneas Sylvius we have a literary counterpart for the exquisite periphrasis of Neroccio's style.

More important, the ideal of feminine beauty summed up in the *Portrait of a Girl* explains the type of the *Madonnas,* which are among Neroccio's most representative and most accomplished works. Of the four paintings of the *Madonna and Child* reproduced in this volume, that at Cracow dates from about 1475 (Plate LXXXVI), and that in Paris from soon after 1480 (Plate LXXXIII), while the Rapolano altarpiece (Plates XC-XCIII), the latest of the series, belongs inside the bracket 1492-6. In the absence of external evidence enabling us to space these paintings over two whole decades, it might be assumed that all of them were painted at an interval of months rather than years and represented one transitory aspect of a prolonged development. It would be wrong, however, to infer from the superficial similarity between the first and last of these *Madonnas* that they reveal a static style, for Neroccio's was an artistic personality which developed at a different speed and under different stimuli to that of other artists. With the exception of one short and far from happy moment of experiment at the close of his career, Neroccio after 1475 was almost impervious to external influence. An artist driven in upon himself, a Narcissus analysing his own image in the pool, his iconography becomes more limited as his style grows more subtle and refined. Assembling the concomitants of his paintings, the lateral Saints, the half-length Virgin and the Child, with the earnest, almost morbid concentration with which later artists were to apply themselves to the properties of their still-lives, Neroccio devised a sequence of ever changing visual harmonies. Each painting is instinct with a new sense of adventure and discovery, and as we turn from one *Madonna* to the next we follow Neroccio in his lonely and laborious ascent to one of the pinnacles of fifteenth century Italian art.

In 1500 Neroccio died. He was survived for less than two years by Francesco di Giorgio and for more than a decade by Benvenuto di Giovanni, but his death in effect marks the close of what is properly called Sienese quattrocento painting. Those of his contemporaries who were able to cast their minds back through the century may have recalled its outstanding achievements, Sassetta's *Scenes from the Life of St. Francis* and Giovanni di Paolo's *Scenes from the Life of St. John,* the frescoes of Domenico di Bartolo and Vecchietta, the *Massacre of the Innocents* of Matteo di Giovanni, the cassone panels of Francesco di Giorgio and Neroccio's altarpieces. If they did so, no doubt they would have commented on the diversity of style of all these works. But today the diversity of fifteenth century Sienese painting is less apparent than its underlying unity, and we are tempted to explain its progress by postulating some form of artistic pre-destination, which ordained that a Sassetta should ultimately be resolved in a Neroccio. Whether it was that Sienese artists did not possess or would not exercise the faculty of aesthetic choice, it cannot be denied that their fidelity to the tradition in which they had been trained lent their work a corporate as well as a personal significance.

Sienese quattrocento painting is a backwater in the stream of artistic evolution. Had Sassetta and Giovanni di Paolo, Francesco di Giorgio and Neroccio never lived, the course of Western painting would not have been materially different from that which it in fact pursued. For this reason Sienese artists of the fifteenth century were long regarded with suspicion and resentment as dilettanti who lacked the moral stamina to make their own small offerings to progress. In a chapter consisting almost exclusively of pejorative comment, Cavalcaselle rejects in turn the panels of Sassetta ('stork-like in the gravity and awkwardness of their motion'), Giovanni di Paolo's 'epileptic vehemence', the frescoes of Domenico di Bartolo ('tasteless dress, stilted movement, and unpleasant masks are common features of his works'), the polyptychs of Vecchietta ('he was nicknamed Vecchietta perhaps because of the tottering frames and aged faces repeated with consistent pertinacity in every one of his works'), the altarpieces of Matteo di Giovanni ('anachronisms of costume are not compensated by taste, nor is the dry bone of form animated into any sort of life'), and the paintings of Benvenuto di Giovanni (the 'reedy frames' of whose figures 'bend affectedly under the weight of large but narrow heads, themselves inclined on slender necks'), while with Francesco di Giorgio and Neroccio the critic's vocabulary is no longer adequate to convey the full range of his disapprobation. The time is past when Cavalcaselle's crude evolutionary standards could pass muster as a serious commentary on Sienese quattrocento painting. Italy no longer convinces the modern traveller as it convinced Charles Dickens 'that the wheel of Time is rolling for an end', and the positivism with which the nineteenth century condemned the Sienese achievement sounds today as the echo of an outworn creed. It is no longer the duty of the art critic to bludgeon the artists of the past for failing to live up to a sense of mission with which they were invested by posterity, nor is it obligatory for the amateur of painting to set up barriers between himself and pictures which can give him inexhaustible delight. It may well be that the elusive beauties of Sienese quattrocento painting demand a special quality of unprejudiced attention, but to those who are prepared to accept the pictures illustrated in this book as the ideal concepts they were designed to be, the artists of the quattrocento, with their purity, refinement and restraint, with the sustained beauty of their images and the fastidious elegance of their technique, must become a source of pleasure as elevated and as lasting as any to be gained from Western art.

FIG. 10. *Sano di Pietro: The Redeemer (Private Collection)*

NOTES ON PLATES

SASSETTA (*ca.* 1400-1450)

Plates I-V: THE MADONNA OF THE SNOW (Conte A. Contini-Bonacossi, Florence).

Dimensions: 241 × 223 cm.

It is known from documentary sources that the painting, which was commissioned by a private donor for the Chapel of S. Bonifazio in the Duomo at Siena, was begun on March 25th, 1430, and completed by mid-October, 1432. The legend of the Miracle of the Snow, which tells how in the year 352 a Roman patrician received a vision of the Virgin bidding him build a church on a site to be recognised from a fall of snow and found the plan of S. Maria Maggiore marked in snowflakes on the ground, is shown in the predella of the altarpiece. In Siena the subject of the Madonna of the Snow occurs not infrequently in the last quarter of the fifteenth century, and Sassetta's altarpiece, an isolated phenomenon in Siena in the first half of the quattrocento, may be tentatively referred to a recrudescence in the devotion of the Virgin of the Snow about 1430, perhaps connected with the refoundation of S. Maria Maggiore a decade earlier.

Plate VI: THE MEETING OF ST. ANTHONY THE ABBOT AND ST. PAUL THE HERMIT (National Gallery of Art, Washington).

Dimensions: 46·3 × 34·3 cm.

The altarpiece, of which this and the two following panels formed part, is not datable on any but stylistic grounds, nor is it known for what church the paintings were commissioned. The original scheme seems to have provided for ten narrative panels (of which seven have been identified) arranged round a central image of the Saint. The iconography of the scenes illustrated in this and the succeeding plates is based on Cavalca's popular life of St. Anthony the Abbot, the panels showing respectively St. Anthony the Abbot accosted and beaten by devils on his way to visit Paul the Hermit, St. Anthony at the entrance to his cell tempted by the devil in the form of a young girl, and St. Anthony's meeting with St. Paul, to whose cell he is directed by a centaur.

Photo: Courtesy of the National Gallery of Art, Washington.

Plate VII: THE SCOURGING OF ST. ANTHONY (Gallery of Fine Arts, Yale University).

Dimensions: 46·3 × 34·3 cm.

See note to Plate VI (above).

Photo: Courtesy of the Gallery of Fine Arts, Yale University.

Plate VIII: THE TEMPTATION OF ST. ANTHONY (Gallery of Fine Arts, Yale University).

Dimensions: 36·8 × 40 cm.

See note to Plate VI (above).

Photo: Courtesy of the Gallery of Fine Arts, Yale University.

Plates IX-XII: MADONNA AND CHILD WITH SS. JOHN BAPTIST, MICHAEL, NICHOLAS AND MARGARET (S. Domenico, Cortona).

Width: 255 cm. (with frame).

The altarpiece is not documented, and is datable only on stylistic grounds. There is no reason to doubt that the picture was commissioned for the church in which it now stands and where it forms a pendant to an altarpiece executed by Fra Angelico *ca.* 1437.

Plates XIII-XV: THE CHARITY OF ST. FRANCIS (National Gallery, London).

Dimensions: 87·6 × 52 cm.

The altarpiece, of which this and the two following panels formed part, was commissioned for the church of S. Francesco at Borgo San Sepolcro in September, 1437, and was completed in June, 1444. In its original form, the painting consisted of a large frontal panel of *St. Francis in Ecstasy between St. John Baptist and the Bd. Ranieri Rasini* (now in the Berenson Collection), a predella, pinnacles, and eight *Scenes from the Life of St. Francis* arranged in two rows on the back of the altarpiece. It is to these eight scenes that the three panels illustrated belong. The scenes represent respectively *The Charity of St. Francis and St. Francis dreaming of the Celestial City,* based on the accounts of Thomas of Celano and Bonaventure, *The Mystic Marriage of St. Francis,* based on the narrative of Bonaventure, and *The Funeral of St. Francis,* deriving from the *Fioretti.*

Photo: National Gallery, London.

Plates XVI and XVIII: THE FUNERAL OF ST. FRANCIS (National Gallery, London).

Dimensions: 87·6 × 52 cm.

See note to plate XIII (above).

Photo: National Gallery, London.

Plates XVII and XIX: THE MYSTIC MARRIAGE OF ST. FRANCIS (Musée Condé, Chantilly).

Dimensions: 95 × 58 cm.

See note to Plate XIII (above).

Photo: Archives Photographiques.

Plate XX: MADONNA AND CHILD WITH TWO ANGELS (Miss Helen C. Frick, New York).

Dimensions: 41 × 31 cm.

One of Sassetta's latest and most beautiful paintings, the panel

FIGS. 11-12. *Pietro di Giovanni d'Ambrogio: The Crucifixion and St. Catherine of Alexandria in Glory (Musée Jacquemart André, Paris)*

was probably executed after 1445, and certainly postdates the St. Francis altarpiece.

Photo: Courtesy of Miss Helen C. Frick, New York.

PIETRO DI GIOVANNI D'AMBROGIO
(*active* 1428-1449)

Plate XXI: THE CRUCIFIXION and ST. CATHERINE OF ALEXANDRIA IN GLORY (Musée Jacquemart André, Paris).
Dimensions: 204 × 170 cm.
Dated 1444, the painting is a double sided processional banner. This fact, combined with the appearance of six flagellants in the foreground both of the *Crucifixion* and of the *St. Catherine*, suggests that the work was almost certainly commissioned by one of the religious confraternities which abounded in fifteenth century Siena.
(Plate XXI is a detail of Figure 12.)

GIOVANNI DI PAOLO (1403-1483)

Frontispiece: ST. NICHOLAS OF TOLENTINO SAVING A SHIP AT SEA (John G. Johnson Art Collection, Philadelphia).
Dimensions: 52 × 42 cm.
Along with a panel in the Vienna Kunstakademie, this panel forms part of a predella containing scenes from the legend of the Augustinian saint, Nicholas of Tolentino. The predella, of which no other panel survives, may be dated *ca.* 1456. The

scene is based on the *Vita S. Nicholai Tolentinis* of Pietro da Monte Rubiano.

Photo: Courtesy of the John G. Johnson Art Collection, Philadelphia.

Plates XXII-XXIV: MADONNA AND CHILD IN A LANDSCAPE (Museum of Fine Arts, Boston).
Dimensions: 56 × 42 cm.
On stylistic grounds the picture, which makes use of a motif more commonly met with in Veronese than in Central Italian painting, may be dated *ca.* 1436. A later version of the scheme exists in the Pinacoteca at Siena (No. 206).
Photo: Courtesy of the Museum of Fine Arts, Boston.

Plate XXV: THE TRIUMPH OF DEATH (Biblioteca Communale, Siena).
From an antiphonal illuminated by Giovanni di Paolo *ca.* 1450-60 for the Abbey of Lecceto. The scheme of the miniature is a simplified version of the familiar trecento theme of *The Triumph of Death*, examples of which occur in a fresco by Bartolo di Fredi in S. Francesco at Lucignano and elsewhere.
Photo: Ministero della Pubblica Istruzione.

Plates XXVI-XXVII: PARADISE (Metropolitan Museum, New York).
Dimensions: 45·6 × 40·3.
The panel is probably a fragment from the predella of an altar-

FIG. 13. *Giovanni di Paolo: St. John Baptist entering the Wilderness*
(Art Institute of Chicago)

piece executed in 1445 for the church of S. Domenico, Siena. In its entirety the predella consisted of two lateral panels of *The Creation* and *The Flood,* and three central panels showing from left to right *Paradise, The Last Judgement* and *Hell.* The panel of *The Creation* survives in the Lehman Collection, New York. A later parallel for the three central panels is provided by a predella of the same subject executed *ca.* 1465, now in the Pinacoteca at Siena.

Photo: Courtesy of the Metropolitan Museum, New York.

Plates XXVIII-XXX: ECCE AGNUS DEI (Art Institute of Chicago).

Dimensions: 68 × 38 cm.

Along with the panel of *St. John Baptist entering the Wilderness,*

reproduced in Fig. 13, the panel forms part of a series of *Scenes from the Life of St. John.* This series seems originally to have been composed of twelve panels, of which six are now in the Art Institute of Chicago, two are at the Landesmuseum at Munster, one is in the Lehman collection, New York, one in the Carvallo collection at Tours and two are lost. Internal evidence suggests that the panels were divided between two mobile wings enclosing a large panel or statue of the Saint. The altarpiece appears to have been painted in the bracket 1455-1460.

Photo: Courtesy of the Art Institute of Chicago.

Plates XXXI-XXXII: THE BIRTH OF ST. JOHN BAPTIST (National Gallery, London).

Dimensions: 30·4 × 36·8 cm.

Along with the scene reproduced on Plates XXXIII-IV, the panel forms part of a predella of *Scenes from the Life of St. John Baptist,* of which four panels are in the National Gallery. The predella, which would originally have consisted of five scenes, appears to have been painted immediately after the Chicago altarpiece, and two of the National Gallery panels, the *St. John entering the Wilderness* and the *Salome with the Head of St. John Baptist* (Fig. 14), are adaptations of similar compositions at Chicago. In both cases the scheme of the *Salome with the Head of St. John Baptist* is based on the relief of the same subject by Donatello on the font in the Baptistery of San Giovanni in Siena.

Photo: National Gallery, London.

Plates XXXIII-XXXIV: ST. JOHN BAPTIST ENTERING THE WILDERNESS (National Gallery, London).

Dimensions: 30·4 × 48·2 cm. (including floriated borders).

See note to Plate XXXI (above).

Photo: National Gallery, London.

FIG. 14. *Giovanni di Paolo: Salome with the Head of St. John Baptist*
(National Gallery, London)

Plate XXXV: St. JEROME (Museo dell' Opera del Duomo, Siena).

Dimensions: 205 × 91 cm.

A very late painting, perhaps executed *ca.* 1475, the *St. Jerome* is evidently an independent votive panel and not the wing of a polyptych. It is characteristic of the harsh, sometimes grotesque work of Giovanni di Paolo's final phase.

SANO DI PIETRO (1406-1481)

Plate XXXVI: St. JEROME BEFORE A CRUCIFIX (Pinacoteca, Siena).

Dimensions: 36 × 27 cm.

An early work, probably executed shortly before 1440.

Plate XXXVII: MADONNA AND CHILD WITH FOUR ANGELS (Osservanza, Siena).

A mature work, perhaps painted *ca.* 1455, the painting is part of a dismembered polyptych, the other panels of which cannot now be re-integrated. At some comparatively recent date the painting was enlarged by the addition of lateral strips of wood, the figures of the angels being completed to right and left of the upper arch. The present reproduction shows the painting in its original form.

DOMENICO DI BARTOLO (*ca.* 1400-1447)

Plate XXXVIII: MADONNA OF HUMILITY (Pinacoteca, Siena).

Dimensions: 93 × 59 cm.

Dated 1433. Apart from its stylistic importance, the painting has a special iconographical interest; it will be noted *inter alia* that the inscription on the cartellino at the base includes the words O STELLA SUPREMI ETERIS, and that that above the Virgin's head includes the words AVE STELLA MICANS, while a star ornamented with tripetalled leaves, representing the Trinity, appears in the upper part of the painting. The use of this motif, which has long-standing liturgical sanction (e.g. the hymn 'Ave Maris Stella'), is comparable to the use of the motif of snow in Sassetta's *Madonna of the Snow* with its reminiscence of St. Bernard's 'Maria nive candidior'.

Plate XXXIX: MADONNA AND CHILD BEFORE A HEDGE OF ROSES (John G. Johnson Art Collection, Philadelphia).

Dimensions: 51·2 × 34·7 cm.

Dated 1437. The use of the motif of a hedge of roses behind the central group is North Italian in origin and goes back to the Yale *Madonna* of Gentile da Fabriano.

Photo: Courtesy of the John G. Johnson Art Collection, Philadelphia.

Plates XL-XLI: THE NURTURE AND MARRIAGE OF THE FOUNDLINGS (Spedale della Scala, Siena).

Commissioned by the rector of the Spedale della Scala, Giovanni di Francesco Buzzicchelli, the frescoes in the Pellegrinaio (the room in which patients would in the fifteenth century have been received by the hospital authorities) were begun in 1441 and completed by January, 1444. It was enjoined in the statutes of the Hospital that foundlings should be cared for at the Hospital's expense and committed to the care of nurses selected by the Hospital. This forms the subject of the left half of the fresco. It was also enjoined that on reaching an appropriate age, the girl foundlings should be encouraged to marry, and on marriage should be presented with 'cinquanta libri de denari senesi' from the funds of the Hospital. A wedding solemnised under these auspices is depicted in the right half of the fresco.

Photo: Courtesy of the Frick Art Reference Library.

(Plates XL and XLI are details of Figure 15.)

FIG. 15. *Domenico di Bartolo: The Nurture and Marriage of the Foundlings (Spedale della Scala, Siena)*

Plates XLII-XLIII: THE DISTRIBUTION OF ALMS TO THE POOR (Spedale della Scala, Siena).

It was also enjoined under the statutes of the Hospital that whole loaves of bread should be distributed weekly to the poor, a ceremony represented in the right half of the present fresco. This, however, is incidental to the main subject of the fresco, which seems to show not the feeding of the poor, but the reception of a novice by the community.

Photo: Courtesy of the Frick Art Reference Library.

(Plates XLII and XLIII are details of Figure 16.)

VECCHIETTA (*ca.* 1412-1480)

Plate XLIV: St. CATHERINE OF SIENA (Palazzo Pubblico, Siena).

FIG. 16. *Domenico di Bartolo: The Distribution of Alms to the Poor (Spedale della Scala, Siena)*

An inscription below the figure records that the fresco was designed to commemorate the canonisation of St. Catherine of Siena by Pope Pius II in June, 1461. Documents, however, suggest that the fresco may have been commissioned as early as the preceding year. A fresco of S. Bernardino had been executed in the same room on the saint's canonisation in the year 1450 by Sano di Pietro.

Plates XLV-XLVII: The Wood of the Suicides and The Earthly Paradise (British Museum, London).
From a manuscript of the *Divine Comedy,* formerly in the Yates-Thompson collection, illuminated for Alfonso of Aragon, probably between 1438 and 1444. The illustrations to the *Paradiso* are by Giovanni di Paolo, while those to the *Inferno* and *Purgatorio* may be attributed with some confidence to Vecchietta. The reproductions illustrate respectively *Inferno,* xiii, l. 31-4, and *Purgatorio,* xxvii, l. 92-3.
Photo: Courtesy of the Warburg Institute.

Plate XLVIII: Madonna and Child with six Saints (Uffizi, Florence).
Dimensions: 156 × 230 cm.
Signed and dated 1457. The Saints are Bartholomew, James and Eligius in the left wing, and Andrew, Laurence and Dominic in the right. Despite this somewhat unusual combination of figures, it has not proved possible to trace for what church or altar the painting was designed. The open-work throne on which the Virgin is seated is reminiscent of that used by Domenico Veneziano in the Carnesecchi *Madonna* in the National Gallery, a painting which Vecchietta may well have known.

Plate XLIX: The Assumption of the Virgin (Duomo, Pienza).
Vecchietta's altarpiece belongs with a series of paintings com-

missioned by Pope Pius II for the newly built Cathedral at Pienza in the years 1461 and 1462. Other polyptychs of the series were executed by Giovanni di Paolo, Sano di Pietro and Matteo di Giovanni. It has been suggested with some plausibility that the figure of St. Pius in the left wing of Vecchietta's *Assumption* is a portrait of Pope Pius II. In contrast to the sometimes perfunctory framing of Sienese fifteenth century altarpieces, the panels are set in a heavy architectural frame, no doubt designed by the artist himself and conceived as an integral part of an aesthetic whole. Indeed the heavy relief of the frame may be compared to the painted niche behind the Palazzo Pubblico *St. Catherine* in that it accentuates the three-dimensional properties of the painting.

THE MASTER OF THE OVILE ANNUNCIATION (active *ca.* 1440-1450)

Plates L-LIII: St. John Baptist and S. Bernardino (S. Pietro Ovile, Siena).
Dimensions: 168 × 37 cm.
The lateral panels of an altarpiece of *The Annunciation* in the same church, the two panels have been attributed at various times to Domenico di Bartolo and Matteo di Giovanni. Apparently executed *ca.* 1445-1450, they have the characteristics of an independent hand, related more closely to Vecchietta than to Domenico di Bartolo, round which a few other paintings can be grouped.
Photo: R. Soprintendenza all' Arte Medioevale e Moderna, Siena.

MATTEO DI GIOVANNI (1435-1495)

Plate LIV: Madonna and Child with two Angels (Pinacoteca, Buonconvento).
Datable on stylistic grounds *ca.* 1470, the painting comes from the Pieve di S. Lorenzo at Percena, for which it was perhaps executed.
Photo: Courtesy of the Frick Art Reference Library.

Plate LV: Madonna and Child with SS. John Baptist and Michael (Barber Institute, Birmingham).
Dimensions: 59·3 × 41·6 cm.
On stylistic grounds the painting, which was formerly in the Pierpont Morgan Collection, may be dated *ca.* 1490.
Photo: Cooper.

Plates LVI-LX: The Assumption of the Virgin (National Gallery, London).
Dimensions: 331 × 173 cm.
It is not impossible that the painting in the National Gallery is identical with an altarpiece of *The Assumption* by Matteo di Giovanni in the church of S. Eugenio outside Siena, which is recorded as dated 1474. In any event the present painting is

attributable on stylistic grounds to the period *ca.* 1475. The theme of St. Thomas the Apostle catching the girdle of the Virgin as she is taken up to heaven recurs frequently in fourteenth and fifteenth century Sienese painting.
Photo: National Gallery, London.

Plate LXI: The Crucifixion (S. Agostino, Asciano).
The painting is the central panel of the predella of an altarpiece executed for the church of S. Agostino at Asciano at a date prior to 1460.
Photo: Courtesy of the Frick Art Reference Library.

Plates LXII-LXV: The Massacre of the Innocents (S. Agostino, Siena).
Datable in the year 1482. It has repeatedly been claimed that the popularity of the subject of *The Massacre of the Innocents* should be attributed to the massacre at Otranto by the Turks in 1480. The recurrence of the subject at this time, however, is more readily susceptible of a purely liturgical explanation. The head shown in Plate LXIV is usually identified as a self-portrait on the analogy of similar figures in Florentine painting.
Photo: Courtesy of the Frick Art Reference Library.

GUIDOCCIO COZZARELLI (1450-1516)

Plates LXVI-LXVIII: The Annunciation and Flight into Egypt (National Gallery, Washington).
Dimensions: 70 × 58 cm.
The sculptural ornamentation at the base of the panel, which looks forward to motifs used by Marrina in the church of Fontegiusta, suggests a relatively late dating, while the brick buildings in which the main action of the scene takes place are typical of Sienese architecture in the last quarter of the fifteenth century.
Photo: Courtesy of the National Gallery of Art, Washington.

BENVENUTO DI GIOVANNI (1436-1518)

Plate LXIX: The Adoration of the Magi (National Gallery of Art, Washington).
Dimensions: 182 × 137 cm.
At one time incorrectly ascribed to Matteo di Giovanni, the painting is certainly later than the altarpiece of 1479 in the National Gallery in London, and may be placed provisionally *ca.* 1490.
Photo: Courtesy of the National Gallery of Art, Washington.

Plate LXX: S. Bernardino Preaching (Walker Art Gallery, Liverpool).
Dimensions: 29·7 × 76 cm.
The painting is usually ascribed to Vecchietta, though at least one critic has proposed the name of Francesco di Giorgio. Its style, however, and particularly the decorative treatment of the architectural background, is characteristic less of Vecchietta than of the painters who emerged from his *bottega,* and the panel may be tentatively regarded as an early work of Benvenuto di Giovanni executed soon after 1460.
Photo: Courtesy of the Walker Art Gallery, Liverpool.
(Plate LXX is a detail of Figure 17.)

Plates LXXI-LXXII: Madonna and Child with SS. Peter and Nicholas (National Gallery, London).
Dimensions: 167 × 169 cm.
Dated 1479. The provenance of the painting is not known. The type perhaps reflects the style of Benozzo Gozzoli, by whose works at San Gimignano Benvenuto di Giovanni was profoundly influenced.
Photo: National Gallery, London.
(Plate LXXI is a detail of Figure 18.)

FRANCESCO DI GIORGIO (1439-1502)

Plate LXXIII: St. Dorothy and the Child Christ (National Gallery, London).
Dimensions: 33 × 20 cm.

Fig. 17. *Benvenuto di Giovanni: S Bernardino preaching (Walker Art Gallery, Liverpool)*

FIG. 18. *Benvenuto di Giovanni: Madonna and Child with SS. Peter and Nicholas (National Gallery, London)*

Similarities between the scheme of the painting and a Bamberg woodcut of the same subject of *ca.* 1470 have given rise to the very plausible suggestion that the panel is based upon a German prototype. The panel seems to have been executed before 1467. Photo: National Gallery, London.

Plate LXXIV: THE HOLY FAMILY WITH SS. BERNARD AND THOMAS AQUINAS (Pinacoteca, Siena).
Dimensions: 198 × 104 cm.
It is known that the picture was commissioned for the monastery of Monte Oliveto in April, 1475. The identification of the

saints as Bernardino and Ambrose and the monogram on the volume in the lower left corner of the painting are additions by a later hand.

Plate LXXV: THE ANNUNCIATION (Pinacoteca, Siena).
Dimensions: 74 × 48 cm.
The fanciful use of perspective in this painting is in such sharp contrast to the relatively conventional methods used in the Cook *Holy Family* that it is tempting to assume that the scene was intended to be looked at from below. If this be so, it is not impossible that *The Annunciation* was originally one of the upper

FIG. 19. *Neroccio: Anthony and Cleopatra (National Gallery, Washington)*

panels of a polyptych. In this connection it may be noted that both the arched form of the panel and the ribs of black and white marble in the pavement recur in the large *Coronation of the Virgin* in the Pinacoteca at Siena.

Plate LXXVI: MADONNA AND CHILD (Musée de Picardie, Amiens).
Dimensions: 75 × 52 cm.
The painting appears to belong to the period *ca.* 1485-90.
Photo: Archives Photographiques.

Plate LXXVII: THE HOLY FAMILY (The Cook Collection, Richmond).
Dimensions: 23·8 × 22 cm.
The painting occupies a position midway between the illuminated *Holy Family* in an antiphonal at Chiusi and a comparable but rather later painting in the Metropolitan Museum, New York, and may be dated tentatively *ca.* 1465.
Photo: Cooper.

Plate LXXVIII: ATLAS (Kupferstichkabinett, Brunswick).
Dimensions: 33·5 × 33 cm.
A later sheet, datable *ca.* 1490.
Photo: Landesmuseum, Brunswick.

Plate LXXIX: AN ALLEGORY OF FIDELITY (Mogmar Art Foundation, New York).
Dimensions: 125·8 × 75·7 cm.
Datable *ca.* 1485. The identification of the subject is tentative.
Photo: Gray.
(Fig. 20 is a detail of Plate LXXIX.)

Plates LXXX-LXXXI: THE GAME OF CHESS (Metropolitan Museum, New York).
Dimensions: 33·7 × 41·3 cm.
Painted in the decade 1480-90, the panel, in conjunction with a dismembered fragment in the Berenson collection, seems to have formed the frontal section of a chest or box. A further

panel illustrating a scene from the same story is in a Brussels collection. The subject of the panels cannot be identified with any confidence.
Photo: Courtesy of the Metropolitan Museum, New York.

Plate LXXXII: MADONNA AND CHILD (Fogg Museum of Art, Cambridge, Mass.).
Dimensions: 45·7 × 28 cm.
An early painting, executed *ca.* 1470.
Photo: Courtesy of the Fogg Museum of Art.

NEROCCIO (1447-1500)

Plate LXXXIII: MADONNA AND CHILD WITH TWO SAINTS (Louvre, Paris).
Dimensions: 42 × 32 cm.
Photo: Archives Photographiques.

Plate LXXXIV: ST. BENEDICT RECEIVING TOTILA (Uffizi, Florence).
Dimensions: 28 × 193 cm. (three panels including frame).
The three scenes of the predella represent the young St. Benedict mending the broken sieve, St. Benedict in the wilderness, and St. Benedict receiving the Gothic King Totila at Montecassino. The last of the three panels shows Totila kneeling in penitence before the Saint, who has unmasked a ruse whereby in an effort to deceive him the King had been impersonated by a servant.

Plate LXXXV: ANTHONY AND CLEOPATRA (National Gallery of Art, Washington).
Dimensions: 38 × 115 cm.
Sometimes attributed to Francesco di Giorgio, the scene, along with its companion panel of *The Battle of Actium* (also in the National Gallery of Art), is certainly by the young Neroccio. The end panels of the cassone have not been identified.
Photo: Courtesy of the National Gallery of Art, Washington.
(Plate LXXXV is a detail of Figure 19.)

Plate LXXXVI: MADONNA AND CHILD WITH TWO ANGELS (Czartoryski Museum, Cracow).
Dimensions: 60·5 × 42 cm.
Photo: Courtesy of the Czartoryski Museum, Cracow.

Plate LXXXVII: PORTRAIT OF A GIRL (National Gallery of Art, Washington).
At one time incorrectly attributed to Francesco di Giorgio, the painting contains in the lower left and right hand corners respectively the letters A.P. and NER. For this reason the painting has sometimes been regarded as a portrait of Alessandra Piccolomini. Along the lower edge is the inscription QUANTUM HOMINI FAS EST MIRA LICET ASSEQUAR ARTE NIL AGO MORTALIS EMULOR ARTE DEOS.
Photo: Courtesy of the National Gallery of Art, Washington.

Plate LXXXVIII-IX: THE ANNUNCIATION (Gallery of Fine Arts, Yale University).
Dimensions: 49 × 130 cm.
Designed as the lunette of an altarpiece and perhaps based on the lunette of *The Annunciation* above the altarpiece by Vecchietta in the Museum at Pienza. The painting to which the present lunette was attached no longer can be identified. Attempts have frequently been made to trace the hand of Francesco di Giorgio in the architectural setting of the scene, while conceding to Neroccio the two figures of the Virgin and the Annunciatory Angel.
Photo: Courtesy of the Gallery of Fine Arts, Yale University.

Plates XC-XCIII: MADONNA AND CHILD WITH SS. SIGISMUND AND ANTHONY THE ABBOT (National Gallery of Art, Washington).
At one time in the Pieve at Rapolano, this altarpiece, perhaps Neroccio's greatest work, can scarcely have been commissioned for a village church, and it is not impossible that the painting, like so many other fourteenth and fifteenth century altarpieces, was presented or sold to a local church by the Sienese church for which it had been designed. The dating of the picture in the 1490's is based on stylistic evidence, and particularly on the manifest connection of the picture with the Montisi altarpiece of 1496.
Photo: Courtesy of the Samuel H. Kress Foundation, New York.

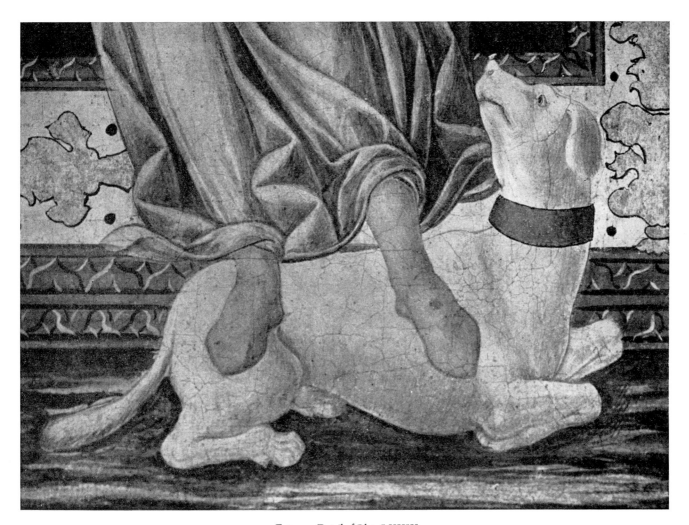

FIG. 20. *Detail of Plate LXXIX*

PLATES

1. SASSETTA: THE MADONNA OF THE SNOW. CONTE A. CONTINI-BONACOSSI, FLORENCE

2. SASSETTA: ST. JOHN BAPTIST, DETAIL FROM THE MADONNA OF THE SNOW.

3. SASSETTA: VIRGIN AND CHILD, DETAIL FROM THE MADONNA OF THE SNOW.

4. SASSETTA: ST. FRANCIS OF ASSISI, DETAIL FROM THE MADONNA OF THE SNOW.

5. SASSETTA: ANGEL KNEADING A SNOWBALL, DETAIL FROM THE MADONNA OF THE SNOW.

6. SASSETTA: THE MEETING OF ST. ANTHONY THE ABBOT AND ST. PAUL THE HERMIT.
NATIONAL GALLERY OF ART, WASHINGTON

7. SASSETTA: THE SCOURGING OF ST. ANTHONY.
GALLERY OF FINE ARTS, YALE UNIVERSITY

8. SASSETTA: THE TEMPTATION OF ST. ANTHONY. GALLERY OF FINE ARTS, YALE UNIVERSITY

9. SASSETTA: MADONNA AND CHILD WITH SS. JOHN BAPTIST, MICHAEL, NICHOLAS AND MARGARET. S. DOMENICO, CORTONA

10. SASSETTA: VIRGIN AND CHILD, DETAIL FROM THE CORTONA POLYPTYCH.

11. SASSETTA: ST. JOHN BAPTIST, DETAIL FROM THE CORTONA POLYPTYCH.

12. SASSETTA: AN ANGEL, DETAIL FROM THE CORTONA POLYPTYCH.

13. SASSETTA: THE CHARITY OF ST. FRANCIS. NATIONAL GALLERY, LONDON

14. SASSETTA: ST. FRANCIS DREAMING OF THE CELESTIAL CITY, DETAIL FROM THE CHARITY OF ST. FRANCIS.

15. SASSETTA: ST. FRANCIS AND THE BEGGAR, DETAIL FROM THE CHARITY OF ST. FRANCIS.

16. SASSETTA: THE FUNERAL OF ST. FRANCIS. NATIONAL GALLERY, LONDON

17. SASSETTA: THE MYSTIC MARRIAGE OF ST. FRANCIS. MUSÉE CONDÉ, CHANTILLY

18. SASSETTA: ST. FRANCIS ON HIS BIER, DETAIL FROM THE FUNERAL OF ST. FRANCIS.

19. SASSETTA: ST. FRANCIS AND THE LADY POVERTY, DETAIL FROM THE MYSTIC MARRIAGE OF ST. FRANCIS.

20. SASSETTA: MADONNA AND CHILD WITH TWO ANGELS. MISS HELEN C. FRICK, NEW YORK

21. PIETRO DI GIOVANNI D'AMBROGIO: ST. CATHERINE, DETAIL FROM ST. CATHERINE OF
ALEXANDRIA IN GLORY. (cp. fig. 12)

22. GIOVANNI DI PAOLO: MADONNA AND CHILD IN A LANDSCAPE. MUSEUM OF FINE ARTS, BOSTON

23. GIOVANNI DI PAOLO: VIRGIN AND CHILD, DETAIL FROM THE MADONNA AND CHILD IN A
LANDSCAPE.

24. GIOVANNI DI PAOLO: LANDSCAPE, DETAIL FROM THE MADONNA AND CHILD IN A LANDSCAPE.

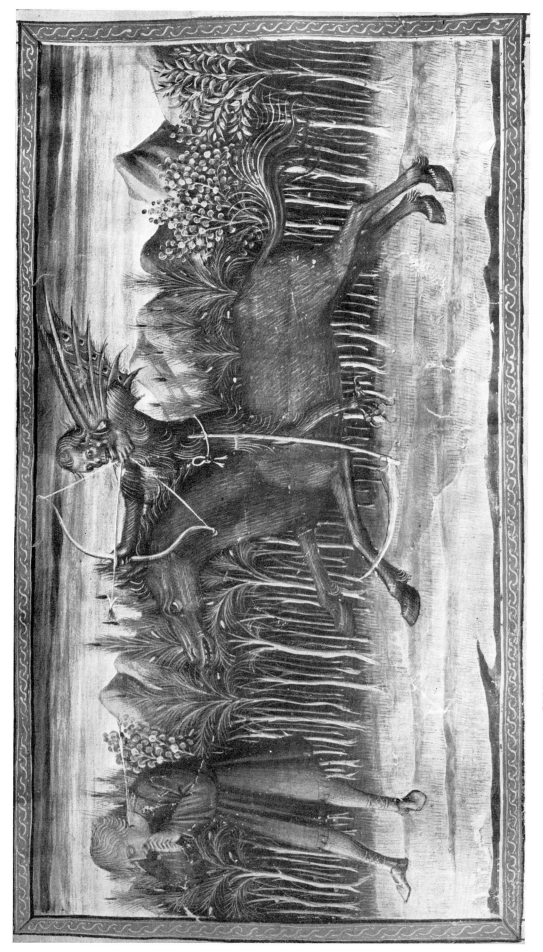

25. GIOVANNI DI PAOLO: THE TRIUMPH OF DEATH. BIBLIOTECA COMMUNALE, SIENA

26. GIOVANNI DI PAOLO: PARADISE. METROPOLITAN MUSEUM, NEW YORK

27. GIOVANNI DI PAOLO: THE BLESSED RECEIVED IN PARADISE, DETAIL FROM THE PARADISE.

28. GIOVANNI DI PAOLO: ECCE AGNUS DEI. ART INSTITUTE OF CHICAGO

29. GIOVANNI DI PAOLO: ST. JOHN BAPTIST, DETAIL FROM ECCE AGNUS DEI.

30. GIOVANNI DI PAOLO: LANDSCAPE, DETAIL FROM ECCE AGNUS DEI.

31. GIOVANNI DI PAOLO: THE BIRTH OF ST. JOHN BAPTIST. NATIONAL GALLERY, LONDON

32. GIOVANNI DI PAOLO: ST. ELIZABETH IN BED, DETAIL FROM THE BIRTH OF ST. JOHN BAPTIST.

33. GIOVANNI DI PAOLO: ST. JOHN BAPTIST ENTERING THE WILDERNESS. NATIONAL GALLERY, LONDON

34. GIOVANNI DI PAOLO: LANDSCAPE, DETAIL FROM ST. JOHN BAPTIST ENTERING
THE WILDERNESS.

35. GIOVANNI DI PAOLO: ST. JEROME. MUSEO DELL'OPERA DEL DUOMO, SIENA

36. SANO DI PIETRO: ST. JEROME BEFORE A CRUCIFIX. PINACOTECA, SIENA

37. SANO DI PIETRO: MADONNA AND CHILD WITH FOUR ANGELS.
OSSERVANZA, SIENA

38. DOMENICO DI BARTOLO: MADONNA OF HUMILITY. PINACOTECA, SIENA

39. DOMENICO DI BARTOLO: MADONNA AND CHILD BEFORE A HEDGE OF ROSES.

40. DOMENICO DI BARTOLO: NURSES TENDING THE FOUNDLINGS, DETAIL FROM THE NURTURE AND MARRIAG
OF THE FOUNDLINGS. (cf. fig. 15)

41. DOMENICO DI BARTOLO: AN ORPHAN CHILD COMMITTED TO ITS FOSTERMOTHER, DETAIL FROM THE NURTURE AND MARRIAGE OF THE FOUNDLINGS.

42. DOMENICO DI BARTOLO: THE CLOTHING OF A NOVICE, DETAIL FROM THE DISTRIBUTION
OF ALMS TO THE POOR. (cf. fig. 16)

43. DOMENICO DI BARTOLO: A MOTHER WITH HER CHILDREN, DETAIL FROM THE DISTRIBUTION OF
ALMS TO THE POOR.

44. VECCHIETTA: ST. CATHERINE OF SIENA. PALAZZO PUBBLICO, SIENA

45. VECCHIETTA: THE WOOD OF THE SUICIDES. BRITISH MUSEUM, LONDON

46. VECCHIETTA: THE EARTHLY PARADISE. BRITISH MUSEUM, LONDON

47. VECCHIETTA: DANTE ASLEEP, DETAIL FROM THE EARTHLY PARADISE.

48. VECCHIETTA: MADONNA AND CHILD WITH SIX SAINTS. UFFIZI, FLORENCE

49. VECCHIETTA: THE ASSUMPTION OF THE VIRGIN. DUOMO, PIENZA

50-51. THE MASTER OF THE OVILE ANNUNCIATION: ST. JOHN BAPTIST AND
S. BERNARDINO. S. PIETRO OVILE, SIENA

52. THE MASTER OF THE OVILE ANNUNCIATION: ST. JOHN BAPTIST.

53. THE MASTER OF THE OVILE ANNUNCIATION: S. BERNARDINO.

54. MATTEO DI GIOVANNI: MADONNA AND CHILD WITH TWO ANGELS.
PINACOTECA, BUONCONVENTO

55. MATTEO DI GIOVANNI: MADONNA AND CHILD WITH SS. JOHN BAPTIST AND MICHAEL.
BARBER INSTITUTE, BIRMINGHAM

56. MATTEO DI GIOVANNI: THE ASSUMPTION OF THE VIRGIN.
NATIONAL GALLERY, LONDON

57. MATTEO DI GIOVANNI: THE VIRGIN, DETAIL FROM THE ASSUMPTION OF THE VIRGIN.

59. MATTEO DI GIOVANNI: ST. THOMAS, DETAIL FROM THE ASSUMPTION OF THE VIRGIN.

60. MATTEO DI GIOVANNI: CHRIST IN GLORY, DETAIL FROM THE ASSUMPTION OF THE VIRGIN.

61. MATTEO DI GIOVANNI: THE CRUCIFIXION. S. AGOSTINO, ASCIANO

62. MATTEO DI GIOVANNI: THE MASSACRE OF THE INNOCENTS. S. AGOSTINO, SIENA

63. MATTEO DI GIOVANNI: AN ATTENDANT, DETAIL FROM THE MASSACRE OF THE INNOCENTS.

64. MATTEO DI GIOVANNI: SELF PORTRAIT, DETAIL FROM THE MASSACRE OF THE INNOCENTS.

65. MATTEO DI GIOVANNI: AN EXECUTIONER, DETAIL FROM THE MASSACRE OF THE INNOCENTS.

66. GUIDOCCIO COZZARELLI: THE ANNUNCIATION AND FLIGHT INTO EGYPT.
NATIONAL GALLERY OF ART, WASHINGTON

67. GUIDOCCIO COZZARELLI: THE ANNUNCIATION, DETAIL FROM THE ANNUNCIATION AND
FLIGHT INTO EGYPT.

68, GUIDOCCIO COZZARELLI: THE FLIGHT INTO EGYPT, DETAIL FROM THE ANNUNCIATION AND
FLIGHT INTO EGYPT.

69. BENVENUTO DI GIOVANNI: THE ADORATION OF THE MAGI. NATIONAL GALLERY OF ART, WASHINGTON

70. BENVENUTO DI GIOVANNI: S. BERNARDINO, DETAIL FROM S. BERNARDINO PREACHING.
(cf. fig. 17)

71. BENVENUTO DI GIOVANNI: VIRGIN AND CHILD, DETAIL FROM
THE MADONNA AND CHILD WITH SS. PETER AND NICHOLAS.
(cf. fig. 18)

72. BENVENUTO DI GIOVANNI: AN ANGEL, DETAIL FROM THE MADONNA AND CHILD
WITH SS. PETER AND NICHOLAS.

73. FRANCESCO DI GIORGIO: ST. DOROTHY AND THE CHILD CHRIST.
NATIONAL GALLERY, LONDON

74. FRANCESCO DI GIORGIO: THE HOLY FAMILY WITH SS. BERNARD AND THOMAS AQUINAS.
PINACOTECA, SIENA

75. FRANCESCO DI GIORGIO: THE ANNUNCIATION. PINACOTECA, SIENA

76. FRANCESCO DI GIORGIO: MADONNA AND CHILD. MUSÉE DE PICARDIE, AMIENS

77. FRANCESCO DI GIORGIO: THE HOLY FAMILY. THE COOK COLLECTION, RICHMOND

78. FRANCESCO DI GIORGIO: ATLAS. KUPFERSTICHKABINETT, BRUNSWICK

79. FRANCESCO DI GIORGIO: AN ALLEGORY OF FIDELITY. MOGMAR ART FOUNDATION, NEW YORK

80. FRANCESCO DI GIORGIO: THE GAME OF CHESS. METROPOLITAN MUSEUM, NEW YORK

81. FRANCESCO DI GIORGIO: TWO CHESS PLAYERS, DETAIL FROM THE GAME OF CHESS.

82. FRANCESCO DI GIORGIO: MADONNA AND CHILD. FOGG MUSEUM OF ART, CAMBRIDGE, MASS.

83. NEROCCIO: MADONNA AND CHILD WITH TWO SAINTS. LOUVRE, PARIS

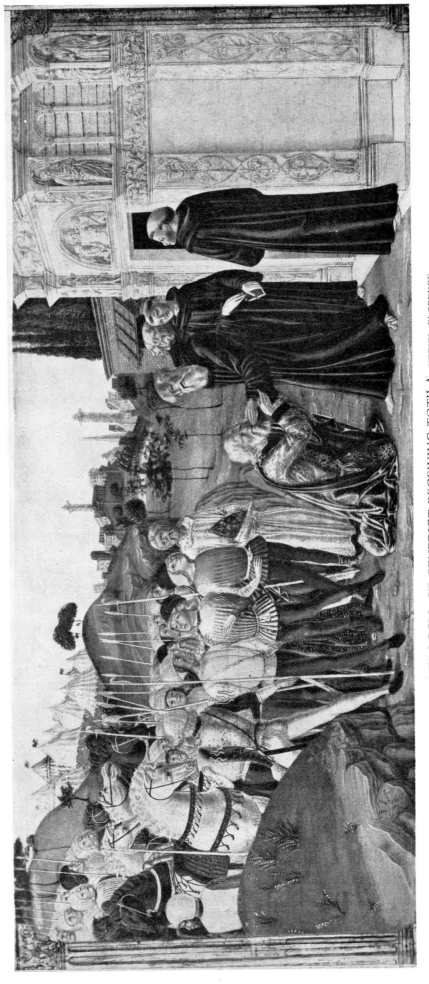

84. NEROCCIO: ST. BENEDICT RECEIVING TOTILA. UFFIZI, FLORENCE

85. NEROCCIO: THE BARGE OF CLEOPATRA, DETAIL FROM ANTHONY AND CLEOPATRA. (cf. fig. 19)

86. NEROCCIO: MADONNA AND CHILD WITH TWO ANGELS. CZARTORYSKI MUSEUM, CRACOW

QVANTVM·HOMINI·FAS·EST·MIRA·LICET·ASSEQVAR·ARTE
NIL·AGO·MORTALIS·EMVLOR·ARTE·DEOS·

87. NEROCCIO: PORTRAIT OF A GIRL. NATIONAL GALLERY OF ART, WASHINGTON

88. NEROCCIO: THE ANNUNCIATORY ANGEL, DETAIL FROM THE ANNUNCIATION.
GALLERY OF FINE ART, YALE UNIVERSITY

89. NEROCCIO: THE VIRGIN ANNUNCIATE, DETAIL FROM THE ANNUNCIATION.
GALLERY OF FINE ART, YALE UNIVERSITY

90. NEROCCIO: MADONNA AND CHILD WITH SS. SIGISMUND AND ANTHONY THE ABBOT.
NATIONAL GALLERY OF ART, WASHINGTON

91. NEROCCIO: VIRGIN AND CHILD, DETAIL FROM THE MADONNA AND CHILD WITH
SS. SIGISMUND AND ANTHONY THE ABBOT.

92. NEROCCIO: ST. ANTHONY THE ABBOT, DETAIL FROM THE MADONNA
AND CHILD WITH SS. SIGISMUND AND ANTHONY THE ABBOT.

93. NEROCCIO: ST. SIGISMUND, DETAIL FROM THE MADONNA AND CHILD WITH
SS. SIGISMUND AND ANTHONY THE ABBOT.

INDEX OF COLLECTIONS

INDEX OF COLLECTIONS